Letting Go

Letting God

30
Day
Devotional
for Moms of
College Freshmen

Contents

Copyright Page 3

Dedication Page..4

Preface...5

Day 1 Shyness 7

Day 2 Friends..9

Day 3 Organization..11

Day 4 Vocation 13

Day 5 Embarrassment... 15

Day 6 Communication 17

Day 7 Faith.. 19

Day 8 Responsibility 21

Day 9 Protection..23

Day 10 Hygiene...25

Day 11 Fear... 27

Day 12 Purity 29

Day 13 Sleep... 31

Day 14 Serving..33

Day 15 Homework 35

Day 16 Loneliness...37

Day 17 Money 39

Day 18 Activeness... 41

Day 19 Church 43

Day 20 Food 45

Day 21 Obedience 47

Day 22 Peace...49

Day 23 Safety 51

Day 24 Health...53

Day 25 Mentor..55

Day 26 Perseverance 57

Day 27 Partying 59

Day 28 Adventures.. 61

Day 29 Professors..63

Day 30 Home 65

Contact...67

Acknowledgements 67

Letting Go Letting God: 30 Day Devotional for Moms of College Freshmen

Copyright © 2019 Jena Stephans

Lettinggolettinggod.com

Cover by Jena Stephans

For Center for Collegiate Mental Health research report mentioned, visit https://ccmh.psu.edu/publications/

This book is dedicated to every mom who feels like a piece of her heart left for college with her freshman. May you find comfort in knowing you are not alone.

Preface

My husband I have sent four of our six children off to college, so I understand the roller coaster of emotions that goes along with it. I was not at all prepared for the deluge of salty water that refused to contain itself in my eyes when my firstborn became a senior in high school. I thought I was excited about this milestone. I mean, after surviving parenting my first teenager, I should have been jumping for joy when the battle of wills was approaching an end, right? Nope. When I first received an email from school explaining senior pictures, college decisions, final yearbook quotes, and a multitude of other things that I couldn't read through my blurred, teary vision, I realized it was going to be much more difficult than I ever imagined. The anticipation of him leaving was like a snowball I had no control of stopping... rolling and growing as it approached the bottom of the hill, which was the day he left with my husband to drive the 800 miles to his new home. Sigh.

I would love to say it gets easier with each child, but for me it did not. Not to be a negative Nancy or anything, but it would be like me saying natural childbirth gets easier with each kid. Trust me, it doesn't. The raw emotions that stem from sending our baby birds out to fly cling to our parental hearts with a fierce grip. Although these emotions start over with the second, third, or sixth child, with each passing day that a child is at college, it does get better as those heart strings become a little more elastic. The hope comes in the way we cope.

My coping mechanism is distraction. I find things to keep my mind busy, so I don't have to focus on the difficult situations in front of me. When my kids left for college, loneliness overcame me, even though I still had a house full of people. I felt helpless and out of control. I couldn't protect my kids from the things I knew they were going to face that might be uncomfortable for them. Then it hit me. "Do not be anxious about anything" (Phil. 4:6a). Of course! God is in control, and I'm not supposed to be. I found a way to turn my fears and worries into a productive distraction— prayer. Praying for the specific things I am concerned about for my children almost immediately eases my senseless and sin-filled worry. Our Heavenly Father understands and wants us to cry out to Him. When I'm praying for my kids, I am letting go of my worries and fears concerning them, and I'm letting God have control. It brings me closer to Him and brings me comfort.

This book will help you get through the first 30 days of having a new college student. Each day has a different topic for you to pray about every time you think of your child. I hope you find that focusing on one area daily will ease your worry, be a blessing for your student, and bring you closer to Jesus.

You will notice that I use the words "kids" and "child/children" frequently. Of course, I know most college students are young adults, but my children will always be my children, regardless of their ages. Since this devotional is meant for parents, I'm not concerned about our kids taking offense to my Mama wording. I'm sure you can relate.

Day 1

"Have I not commanded you? Be strong and courageous. Do not be frightened, and do not be dismayed, for the Lord your God is with you wherever you go."
~ Joshua 1:9 ~

SHYNESS

One of the biggest concerns I had the first day my kids were at college was that they would sit in their dorm rooms during all the get-to-know-you activities, too shy or nervous to meet new people. In my Mama head, I could just picture them sitting there all alone on their phones scrolling through videos, giving occasional longing glances out the window into crowds of freshmen all laughing and making new friends. Of course, that wasn't the reality, but I had a hard time seeing them as the ones in the crowds bonding.

Different colleges have different ways of engaging incoming freshmen, but most do a pretty good job of encouraging (or even requiring) them to participate in a multitude of events. The more activities they do, the more they will get to know other newbies. For most of my kids, the friendships they formed that first week were their stable relationships throughout their freshmen years (and beyond). It is not easy for many young adults to get out of their comfort zones, though, and unless they are the type who knocks on new neighbors' doors without you telling them they must, they probably need a little encouragement. It's okay to reach out (within reason...texting every half hour asking if everything is okay, is NOT a good idea). Your freshman will be happy to know you didn't forget about him already and glad to have the chance to share concerns.

Be sure to get ahold of the Welcome Week schedule planned for incoming freshmen. With social media and college websites, it is usually not too difficult to attain, even if your child didn't willingly share it with you (but ask him for it first – you may be surprised). We all know parents have incredible sleuthing skills, so now is the time to use them. Send strategic texts an hour or so before the activities that you know will involve smaller groups (Bible studies, scavenger hunts, ice cream socials, etc.) and ask your student what he is doing, if he is having fun, etc. If the reply is that he doesn't want or need to, then it's time to try to persuade him to grab that new roommate and venture out and be brave. Mention that you know how difficult it is, with the assurance that the friendships will follow because almost everybody is in the same boat with similar feelings...just like the parents who sent off their kids to college. It does get easier.

Lord, please help _____ to be assertive and to participate in lots of activities this week. Help him meet people, start forming positive relationships, and resist the comfort of being shy. Please remove any nervous feelings he may have. In Jesus's name, amen.

Day 2

"Do not be deceived: 'Bad company ruins good morals.'"
~ 1 Corinthians 15:33 ~

FRIENDS

You've got this! I remember when I started kindergarten, my mom sent me with snacks that were meant for sharing to help ease the awkwardness of initiating conversations with complete strangers. We all want our kids to have friends, and it's probably unanimous that parents want them to be chosen with discernment. When my kids were little, it was somewhat difficult for me to explain the importance of surrounding oneself with positive, Christ-loving relationships without excluding those who need to have somebody to be the light for them. I wanted them to be able to go to little Suzy's or Bobby's house, knowing they would pray before meals and not watch anything on TV besides Veggie Tales. Peace of mind for Mama. I did encourage those types of friendships at an early age to help them avoid difficult morality choices and negative influences when they were still learning right from wrong, but I hoped as they got older that they would gravitate towards those bonds (on a more mature level) on their own.

Many friends are made during the first week of college, and I prayed a lot my kids would choose them wisely. The first person your freshman will likely meet is her roommate. She could be a lifelong friend or an acquaintance only seen for a semester; hopefully, they can help each other get through the first few weeks and beyond. This is the time for you to give your child the CRU or FCA information for her college and some website links to local churches that have small groups for young adults. She will be more likely to grasp the concept that it's a good idea when she doesn't know many people yet, but has the desire to belong. Remind her it's important for all of us to have a few close friends who will help us with accountability.

Beyond just surrounding themselves with friends who value Christian morals and will obey the law, we also want our kids to not exclude loving those who don't. As much as it is in my Mama comfort zone for them to only have Veggie-Tales and Adventures in Odyssey friends, I know that God also wants them to be like Jesus and befriend all types of people who need to be loved.

As you think of your child today as she forms new friendships, pray for strong, positive bonds and that she will reach out to others who also could use a friend. Perhaps send her a big box of ice-pops she can put in her freezer and share with her suite mates, hall, orientation group, etc. Kindergarten wasn't that long ago, after all.

Lord, help _____ to be discerning when choosing her friends. Help her to surround herself with people who are positive influences and followers of You. Help her be a light and a friend to those who need it and not waiver in her faith or be ashamed of it. In Jesus's name, amen.

Day 3

"But all things should be done decently and in order."
~ 1 Corinthians 14:40 ~

ORGANIZATION

Each of my children's levels of organization has varied and changed over the years. Growing up, one of my daughters kept her room cleaner than her siblings. She had a labeled bin for everything and rarely was there clutter on her floor. When she returned for the first long weekend at home after leaving for college, I was dumbfounded at the amount of stuff she left all over the house. It pretty much stayed that way throughout her visits home. She's now married and still leans more towards the carefree attitude where clutter doesn't bother her. If she is planning a trip or scheduling activities for her job, however, her organization skills come to the surface. Her budget is figured out to the penny and even her computer files all have an assigned place. It works well for her and she is successful.

My sons all seem to go through stages of when they are organized and when they aren't. Regardless of their differences, for each of my kids — no matter what grade of school they are entering — the week before school is spent organizing school supplies and planning subjects in binders or folders. Sure, that usually changes by the third or fourth week of school when papers get stuffed into books, but at least it's a start. That same anticipation carries over into college. It might not be easy finding the assignments online and keeping a digital calendar (Do they even know what a paper one is?), but I can assure you they figure it out. It might not be how you or I would do it, but they all seem to do what works for them.

One of my sons is excellent with Excel spreadsheets, so he keeps all his information in different spreadsheets. My college-graduate son liked to write things down (yep — old fashioned pen and paper), and the one who is starting his sophomore year of college relies on the university's website reminders. So, as you think of your child's high school locker being packed full of books wedged into the pages of other books, with folded papers sticking out and crumpled, and remember the assignments you ran up the day they were due because he left them sitting on the printer (You couldn't let him fail after doing all the work, right?!), know that he will be okay and he will finally be able to figure out how to do it all by himself the best way that works for him — not you or the high school guidance counselor. Remember all those books you read (and if you're like me, completely ignored) that told you to let your children learn from their mistakes and not to rescue them every time they needed help? Well, now you don't have a choice, so he really will learn quickly to take care of himself.

Lord, please help _____ to be organized and understand the importance of it so he can keep track of his assignments and classes. Help him to seek advice if necessary and find whatever methods are most beneficial for him now and in the future. In Jesus's name, amen.

Day 4

"Having gifts that differ according to the grace given to us, let us use them: if prophecy, in proportion to our faith; if service, in our serving; the one who teaches, in his teaching; the one who exhorts, in his exhortation; the one who contributes, in generosity; the one who leads, with zeal; the one who does acts of mercy, with cheerfulness."
~ Romans 12:6 ~

VOCATION

Some people know what careers they want when they are in the second grade, then actually follow through with their plans; others still don't know what they want to do their fifth year of college, after switching majors four times. When kids choose what career paths they'll venture down, it isn't always easy for parents. What if she is taking classes because of a boyfriend's persuasion? What if she is choosing something requiring activities or accessories you know she can't afford? What if she wants to get into an extremely competitive program in which you know it will be very difficult for her to succeed? Your child's desired vocation may change several times, and she may even switch colleges before she graduates, as God opens and closes doors to guide her.

When my daughter was in high school, she felt called to go to a musical theater conservatory. Due to various reasons, my husband and I did not think it would be a good fit for her. We prayed about it and did not feel at peace. When we told her that her desired school would not be an option, she was seriously considering trying to come up with her own financial resources to go anyway. Confused about if my husband and I were doing the right thing, I talked to a pastor who very wisely told me that God would not put one thing on my husband's and my hearts and then put something different on my daughter's heart. Duh! Why didn't I think of that? He suggested we pray regularly and faithfully separately from our daughter and have her do the same for a couple of months, without bringing it up for discussion at all. During that time, I prayed for direction, clarity, and wisdom for all of us, and tried my best to listen to God. When we reached the decision-making time, my husband and I still felt disturbed and had to tell my daughter she couldn't attend. She was disappointed but ended out selecting a school closer to home and her high school sweetheart. Although it wasn't as specialized and intense as her first choice, she learned a lot, and felt confident that God was using her wherever she was.

The most important thing our kids can do when choosing a vocation, is seek how God wants them to use their gifts, so they can best lead others to Him. We all remember what it was like to be young and carefree and want to make our own decisions. Sometimes parents know what's best and sometimes the young adult does, but God ALWAYS does.

Lord, please lead _____ to a vocation where she can serve You, using the gifts and talents with which You have blessed her. Help me to know when she is following You and trust her decisions. Open doors where they need to be opened so she can do your will. In Jesus's name, amen.

Day 5

"Fear not, for you will not be ashamed; be not confounded, for you will not be disgraced; for you will forget the shame of your youth, and the reproach of your widowhood you will remember no more."
~ Isaiah 54:4 ~

EMBARRASSMENT

There is a reoccurring dream that I have had since I was a young child. In it, I am confused about where I am supposed to be at school, have an important test, and can't find my classroom. I cannot remember the order of my classes, and my schedule has magically gone missing. I try to go to the office for help but can't find that, either. I see people I know and they all seem to be in the right places, leaving me the only one failing and embarrassed. Usually around the time the bell rings (meaning I missed the entire class, test and all), I wake up. It's such an awful feeling!

I find it interesting that I still have that dream as an adult, having graduated from college over 25 years ago. My training in psychology tells me the dream I had as a child because I was afraid of messing something up and being embarrassed starting school, has transferred over into parenthood as I worry about the same situation for my kids. I know, I know — "Do not be anxious about anything" (Philippians 4:6a). I remind myself of that verse often, usually several times a day.

Preparation is extremely beneficial for preventing new college students from losing their way. Not to worry — there are multitudes of people trained to help your child be prepared! All schools have students and faculty devoted to guiding incoming freshmen to where they need to be and to additional resources if they need help locating something. Remember when your child was a freshman in high school and she walked to her classes ahead of time to find them, put her belongings into her locker, and made sure she knew where everything was? She's done the same thing this time. If anything does go wrong, all the professors and faculty totally understand and are helpful and forgiving.

We don't want our children to have to suffer through anything embarrassing, because we remember what it feels like, but we also know that we got over those moments and can laugh about them — well, most of them — now. As you pray for your child today to not have to face anything embarrassing as she starts this new adventure, may you be comforted by knowing that she is in the presence of our Savior...and so are you!

Lord, thank You for always being near to _____ and to me. Please help her to find her classes, to not get lost, to memorize her schedule, and to avoid any kind of embarrassing situations. Help her to use the resources she has available to her. In Jesus's name, amen.

Day 6

"Let your father and mother be glad; let her who bore you rejoice."
~ Proverbs 23:25 ~

COMMUNICATION

With all the different ways to communicate, it's easier than ever before to stay in touch with our college kids. Some are great about daily texts, snaps, calls, or posts, but others are more of the out-of-sight-out-of-mind mentality. The key is to find out how your child likes to communicate and tap in to that, while finding a balance so as not to annoy him. No college student wants his parents calling him in the middle of class every day to make sure he didn't skip it and confirm that he ate breakfast.

When each of my kids left for college, I tried to prepare myself for the lack of communication I expected. Thankfully, they kept in close contact with me completely on their own for at least the first semester, so I can assure you there is hope. They called or texted almost daily. One of my sons knew I liked when he checked in with me when he arrived at friends' houses when he was living at home, so he suggested he permanently share his location with me on our iPhones, so I could just check it when I wanted. Seriously? I was not expecting that, but my Mama heart practically skipped a beat from contentment overload. My boys had SnapChat and I absolutely hated that app but downloaded it in hopes they would include me in their snaps. It worked! I still don't like that I must find random things to take pictures of in order to respond, but I have grown to love seeing what they see as they send pictures. I try to send meaningful pictures back, even if it is just décor that might give them a little glimpse of home. At first, I took lots of screen shots because the pictures disappeared so quickly. My sons texted me and asked why I was taking screen shots of everything they sent. Oops! I didn't know it told the senders when I did that. I explained that I felt like I was missing something, so they changed the time photos appeared to me to infinite. Ha! I'll take it. One of my sons Facetimed me a lot the first semester of college. I love seeing my kids, but I'm not thrilled viewing myself in the corner of the screen. I ignored all my insecurities each time he contacted me, though, because I was excited he initiated communication and I could see his face that I missed so much, along with his dorm room, new fish, roommate, sunsets, and many other things he offered to show me during our conversations.

As my kids got more comfortable away from home and made friends, the initiated communication became less frequent, but they usually responded when I texted. Remember balance — text and wait for a reply, even if you want one immediately. Communication works both ways. Send pictures of the pets or siblings or all of you making a silly face. He may be wishing you reached out to him as much as you are longing for the same from him.

Lord, I am grateful for the many ways we can communicate. Please put it on _____'s heart to keep in touch with me, and help me to also reach out to him as much as he needs me to, without being a burden.
In Jesus's name, amen.

Day 7

"Commit your work to the Lord, and your plans will be established."
~ *Proverbs 16:3* ~

FAITH

Congratulations on surviving your first week without your college student! At this point, your child is getting settled and starting to feel a sense of belonging at her home away from home. As she adjusts to her new friends and schedule, she also will need to figure out her priorities, hopefully putting God at the forefront. It is great for parents to be able to advise their freshmen to stay on course and keep their faith. One of the most difficult parts of being parents of young adults, however, is that we can't force them to do what we want them to anymore. I started feeling that way when the first one hit thirteen.

When they were younger, if I wanted my kids to know the importance of putting Jesus first in everything, I would have just said, "You need to put Jesus first in everything." A toddler response would be, "Okay, Mommy." The four-year-old would say, "Why?" The ten-year-old would respond with, "Do I have to?" (with an "alright" after hearing a "yes" from me). The fourteen-year old would roll both eyes with a sigh and say either, "Duh!" or "Why would I want to do that?" (depending on where she is in her spiritual walk). Our young adults probably know they need to put Jesus first, but they may need reminded...or proof. For them, proof is probably somewhere on the internet...but that's okay because the entire Bible is on the World Wide Web!

I remember when YouTube and Pinterest first became popular. I had always assumed I would be able to share my knowledge of a multitude of areas I excelled at with my kids as they became interested in different subjects and asked for my help. Suddenly, I was replaced with complete strangers. I would offer my assistance on everything from make-up and cooking to building fires and forts, but the responses would be, "Oh, it's okay; I'll just look it up on YouTube," or "I have that pinned already." Really? What ever happened to learning by spending time with people or looking it up together in a book? Shouldn't we learn to bake Great-Grandma's special recipe by actually cooking in the kitchen with family members who learned it first-hand? Shouldn't personal interactions be the best way to grow closer to God? Your child may not think so. Whatever is the most relatable way for her to hear about or share Jesus is okay, even if it's not the same as it was for our generation.

Technology has changed rapidly, and we need to adapt and incorporate it into our parenting. We can help point them in the right direction by sharing videos or pins that are relevant to their ages (and biblically accurate). They seem to thirst for discussions and appreciate different viewpoints. I have a hard time not seeing everything as black and white, but my kids have opened my eyes to some areas that are gray. Some I'm okay with and some I'm not. As parents of adults, we can mentor. We can't force faith upon them, but we can pray. God hears us, and the best part is that He knows not only our hearts, but our kids' hearts, also.

Lord, I want _____ to put You first in all she does because I know that is what You want. Please help her to feel the nudging of the Holy Spirit so she makes You her priority. Help strengthen her relationship with You while she is away. In Jesus's name, amen.

Day 8

"Whatever you do, work heartily, as for the Lord and not for men."
~ Colossians 3:23 ~

RESPONSIBILITY

The original prayer focus word I had for today was "independence." When I started looking into scripture for it, however, I couldn't find much. As I dug a little deeper, I realized that God didn't design people to be independent and the word I was looking for was "responsibility." Ephesians 6:4 says, "Fathers, do not provoke your children to anger, but bring them up in the discipline and instruction of the Lord." We are instructed to guide our children towards having a relationship with Jesus and to follow His teachings, according to the Bible. Instead of hoping they are independent, we must realize that our children need to be dependent upon Christ and responsible in their daily living.

No parent wants their kids to fail, but we are probably all willing to have it happen if it serves a greater purpose which we know will help them succeed. Some of us are more willing than others. I am the type of parent who would much rather help my children avoid disappointment than have them suffer. I have struggled with this since the time they were little. I say "struggled" because my psychology background tells me people learn from their mistakes, and I sometimes have a difficult time knowing when exactly to let them learn or not. You would think that by the sixth child, I would have mastered that concept, but I still run forgotten lunches up to school. I don't want my kids to be hungry. Haven't we, as adults, called our spouses, parents, or teens to help us because of something we overlooked or left at home or locked in the car? Of course, we have! We depend on those who love and care about us to help us. If the help is coming too frequently, though, that is where the line is drawn, and lessons are not being learned. It's all about balance, yet again.

Help your student learn how to use his resources to be successful in college. Be there for him to help him look up things if he needs help and quickly buy a book if he forgot to order it and needs it in a day, but know when his dependence conflicts with his ability to be responsible. If he is "using" you consistently and not doing things on his own that he is perfectly capable of doing, or if his actions of irresponsibility will harm him or others or are unlawful, then it is time to let him learn that you will not be there to bail him out from those types of behaviors. When I'm faced with parenting decisions, I'm reminded how my Heavenly Father is there for me and helps me more times than I can count, yet He also lets me learn from falling and getting back up. Pray your child can be responsible, which includes being dependent upon God.

Lord, today I ask that You help _____ be responsible with his freedom, education, schedule, and time. Guide him to know how to take the initiative to solve problems and be resourceful. Help me know when to step in and offer help and when to let him handle problems on his own. In Jesus's name, amen.

Day 9

"God is our refuge and strength, a very present help in trouble."
~ Psalm 46:1 ~

PROTECTION

One of the things I pray about the most for my kids is protection. I get frustrated when I have no control and need to remind myself constantly that God is control, not me. There is nothing I can do to prevent bad weather, earthquakes, or dangerous animals from approaching. I am not going to like the outcome of every situation, but I know that He is holding on to my children.

My oldest son attended Union University in Jackson, Tennessee. One of the reasons he chose to go all the way to that college (we live in Florida) was that they had awesome dorms. Each student gets a bed and a desk in their own private room! Four suitemates share two bathrooms, a large living area, and a kitchen with a full-size refrigerator and oven. They have some of the best dorms I have ever seen on a Christian college campus. UU was founded in the late 1800's and its current location was built in 1975. So why are the dorms so amazing? Well, four years before my son was a freshman there, an EF-4 tornado ripped through campus, tearing it apart and injuring dozens of students. Miraculously, there were no deaths. Because of the destruction, fourteen new residential buildings were constructed.

Because of the UU tornado, I keep weather alerts on my phone for the counties where my kids attend college. They don't pay much attention to weather warnings, so I figure it can't hurt to send them texts when something dangerous is heading their way. Last spring, I received a notification that Liberty University — where two of my sons attend college — was under a tornado warning. I texted my boys to make sure they knew what was coming. One of my sons replied with, "I know. I'm looking out my window now at ten tornadoes off in the distance." "Really?" I shakily replied, to which he responded, "No, Mom. I'm kidding." Funny. I'm glad they know they can joke about my sometimes-overprotective Mama heart.

I received a call one day from one of my sons asking for advice because he was covered in ticks. Yikes! Of course, I immediately thought of Lyme disease, but we looked up the best way to get rid of them and he was fine. My sons have come close to bears, snakes, alligators, and a multitude of other creatures that could be potentially harmful, but they have also been thrilled with seeing and respecting God's creations.

At the three colleges my kids have attended so far, they have all had alert systems in place. As long as you won't worry unnecessarily each time you get a text, be sure to sign up to receive them on your own phone. If you don't know how, call and ask. I have gotten them about weather, bomb threats, power outages, gas leaks, and suspicious people. They are great reminders for me to pray for the students' safety and those on or near campus trained to handle those situations a lot better than I ever could.

Lord, place a hedge of protection around _____ and keep her safe. Help her know You are with her in all situations. Help me to remember that, too, and be reminded You are in control. In Jesus's name, amen.

Day 10

"Or do you not know that your body is a temple of the Holy Spirit within you, whom you have from God? You are not your own, for you were bought with a price. So glorify God in your body."
~ 1 Corinthians 6:20 ~

HYGIENE

Did you brush your teeth? Did you wash your hands...with soap? Remember to wash behind your ears. Don't forget your belly button. I think you may need a little more deodorant. It's a good idea to shower every day. Those are things I am guessing every parent has said repeatedly. I know I have. It's a little different when our kids become adults because hopefully, they know to do all those things on their own. However, we have all seen plenty of adults who seem to leave out some of the hygiene rituals, and our hope is that it isn't our own kid that is spreading germs.

Of course, the real reason we want our kids to practice healthy hygiene habits is because we want them to be healthy and not sick or suffering from something that could have been prevented. Washing hands prevents everything from the common cold to meningitis. Brushing teeth regularly helps avoid problems with gingivitis, tooth decay, and gum disease. Maintenance and check-ups are less expensive than treatments down the road. I'll admit it...I also don't want my kids to smell of BO or bad breath for the sake of those around them. A dirty belly button won't really grow root vegetables, but it is a little nasty.

Since they are probably still on your insurance, you can help motivate your adult kids by making their regular dentist, eye, and doctor appointments well in advance for times you know they will be home from school. Since dentist visits are usually scheduled every six months, I make one during the summer and one in late December or early January. They might go begrudgingly, but chances are they will go because the appointment is already made.

There is a difference between hygiene and appearance, and we need to remember that as long as we are paying the doctors' bills, we have a right to enforce preventative healthcare measures. However, young adults no longer need us to remind them to do any of the daily hygiene activities. They can take care of themselves, as hard as it may be for us to admit. If your son skips a couple days of showering because he is camping with friends or doesn't brush his teeth because he is too tired, he will be okay...and so will you.

Lord, please help _____ to take care of his body, knowing it is a temple of the Holy Spirit. Help him to be healthy and free from infection, disease, and sickness. Help me to not interfere with his ability to take care of himself, under Your care. In Jesus's name, amen.

Day 11

"...for God gave us a spirit not of fear but of power and love and self-control."

~ 2 Timothy 1:7 ~

FEAR

My senior in high school is currently facing preparations for college — teacher recommendations, scholarship applications, college visits and decisions, music auditions, choices for majors, etc. My other kids were a little nervous about this next chapter of their lives, but they had a sense of excitement and anticipation. My senior, on the other hand, has avoided most things college-related because of her fear of the unknown. I understand that because I, too, am not comfortable with new situations and the "what-ifs" that go through my head when I think about different scenarios. My husband, however, can easily go into any unfamiliar place with people he hasn't met and face new encounters head-on.

Fear can stem from several things, the most common being past circumstances and the unknown. Although there may be fears based on past occurrences that could be triggered while your student is in college, the majority will come from not knowing what to expect because it is all so new to him. It is like being in the dark. I am not a fan of the pitch black unless I am trying to sleep or am playing laser tag. Otherwise, I don't enjoy trying to navigate when I can't see if I'm going to run into something that will make me fall, and I can't help but wonder if something might be there that shouldn't be. If I'm sleeping, my eyes are closed anyway, so bring on the darkness because I know I can't fall.

During the summer months and school breaks, my kids invite friends over and our family plays laser tag in our house...in complete darkness. We turn off all the lights and cover any light sources. Even light coming in the big windows is hidden by blankets. Because we have run through and hidden in all areas, there isn't fear since we know what is there and the guests know they aren't alone. We have had bumps and bruises, scrapes, and even a couple broken bones from running into each other, but we aren't afraid of the dark because we have experienced it so many times and know the fun outweighs the possible problems.

The college experience is scary and unknown for the students who don't know what to expect, but that is why they have college visits and orientation. It prepares them, so they know what is coming before they begin, and they also realize quickly that they aren't alone. Every other freshman is there, too, experiencing the same things. Whatever your freshman was fearing about the first week of school, he has already overcome. With each week, comes less fear. He may be navigating in the dark, but God is the beacon guiding him. As he gets more and more familiar with his surroundings and the expectations, he will find his way and find the fun.

Lord, thank You for being a light in the darkness for _____. Help him to not be afraid and to feel Your presence and comfort. Turn any of his uncertainty into confidence and control. In Jesus's name, amen.

Day 12

"Let no one despise you for your youth, but set the believers an example in speech, in conduct, in love, in faith, in purity."

~ 1 Timothy 4:12 ~

PURITY

There are so many different views today about the roles of men and women that it can be somewhat confusing. Should men hold the door open for ladies, or does that cause a feeling of inadequacy or inferiority? Who should pay for the meal on a date? Is it okay for a girl to ask the boy out? Is dating okay? What about purity? The questions could go on. The culture of today paints a picture of anything goes. Turn on any movie, show, or interview and it is "normal" to see couples living together, marriages happening after having children together, and little regard for respect of the opposite sex. Christ being the center of a relationship is usually only in corny movies young adults wouldn't watch. When people are exposed to something repeatedly, they become desensitized to it. As parents, we need to pray a lot that our kids will feel uncomfortable about the situations that are not honoring to God, so they feel the tugging of the Holy Spirit to follow His guidelines according to scripture and not societal norms.

We want our kids to have healthy relationships and to be appreciated and valued for how God created them and where He leads them. They very possibly could meet their future spouses while at college, so praying for that relationship is also a consideration. During my oldest son's first semester of college, I loved hearing about his group of friends and seeing pictures he would send me as I tried to learn which names went with which faces. One of them was a girl who I heard mentioned quite a bit. When I asked if he liked her as more than a friend, my son told me that he did not. He said that his other friend did, even though the girl did not feel the same way. Eventually, my son admitted to his group of friends that he had developed feelings for the girl. They got upset with him, since the other guy in their friend-group liked her first. It was very difficult for my son because he had to choose between the girl and his friends. He chose the girl, and they got married a couple months after graduating from college. He followed where God led him...to his future wife, even though there were struggles along the way.

Keep the line of communication about friendships and dating open, and don't be afraid to remind your child of the proper way to treat the opposite sex. Bring up modesty, boundaries, and the importance of sexual purity (there is a lot of scripture about this). Warn of the dangers of date rape and explain how to avoid it. Don't be afraid to ask outright about pornography. Encourage having groups of friends to attend outings with for accountability. Most of all, pray throughout the day that your child will remain close to Jesus in temptations and have a pure heart, mind, and body while at college.

Lord, I praise you for the way you designed males and females to be so different, yet so compatible. Please help _____ to avoid temptations involving the opposite sex. Help her to feel the Holy Spirit leading her to set boundaries and follow them. Help her to have respect for her own body and for others and to remain pure in body, mind, and heart for her future spouse. In Jesus's name, amen.

Day 13

"If you lie down, you will not be afraid; when you lie down, your sleep will be sweet."

~ Proverbs 3:24 ~

SLEEP

I remember being in college and staying up late doing homework and socializing with friends. I had nobody telling me what time to go to bed and, being a natural night owl, I stayed up until I got tired — very late. The problem came with the 8:00 a.m. classes. I would make it to them, but sometimes in my pajamas and never with makeup or pretty hair. In class, I'm sure my focus was more on trying to stay awake than on college algebra. College students are extremely sleep deprived. Lack of sleep can lead to minor things like moodiness and lack of concentration, as well as major issues such as lung disease and heart problems.

There seems to be a quick fix for most things nowadays, and the remedy for many college students who are lacking sleep is caffeine...lots of it. Companies who sell drinks with large amounts of it use college students as their targets in marketing campaigns and are very successful at selling to them. Young adults often do not see the potential risks of energy drinks since they are legal and seem so minor compared to illegal drugs or alcohol. As parents, we cannot tell them what to eat and drink and how much caffeine to consume, so we can only pray they will get enough sleep that they won't crave substitutions to give them the energy they need.

During the summers, we have always let our kids sleep until they wake up. We figure they will get up early for the rest of their lives, so they might as well sleep in while they can. When the summer begins, they get up relatively early, as they do when school is in session. As the summer progresses, they stay up later and later at nighttime and the arise time for some of them is often after noon. It doesn't bother me because I stay up late with them and love the laughter and commotion. I am fortunate that my schedule permits me to adjust to their times. Since I have lots of children and they wake up on their own, I can see how each of them

31

requires varying amounts of sleep. If we all go to sleep at the same time, some of us consistently need seven to eight hours, some more like nine or ten. My husband does just fine on six. We all have different times, also, that we naturally get tired.

I can tell you from experience that we don't need to worry as much as we do about them not getting enough sleep. It may take an entire semester or two to adjust to not having Mom or Dad waking them up and telling them to sleep, but I have noticed that as they become more independent and need to wake up for classes or jobs, they learn to figure out how much sleep they need and adjust their sleeping schedules accordingly.

Lord, please allow _____ to have the necessary sleep that his body needs. Help him to manage his time in a way that gives him rest, and help him to rely on exercise and sleep for energy and not unhealthy options. Help me to sleep, knowing he is resting well in Your care. In Jesus's name, amen.

Day 14

"As each has received a gift, use it to serve one another, as good stewards of God's varied grace."
~ Isaiah 54:4 ~

SERVING

In Florida where my kids have all attended high school, there is a state scholarship that requires a minimum number of service hours. I'm assuming other states have similar offers. Students who might not otherwise volunteer are eager to serve others in hopes of a reward for college tuition. I love this because I think many people who haven't served others much have doubts and concerns about things like unthankful people, boredom, getting dirty, being tired, wasting time, or being too busy. One of the neat things about serving others is that it not only benefits those being served, but it also is extremely satisfying for the one doing the serving. The incentives that the states offer encourages teenagers to get a feel for that.

Most Christian universities and some other colleges require students to serve in some capacity. For those that do not, there are numerous opportunities for students to help others on and off campus. They may need a little motivation to make that first step, but after that, they often want to continue to serve on their own. Matthew West wrote a book several years ago called *Give This Christmas Away*. You may have heard the song he and Amy Grant sang with the same title. The book has lots of ideas in it about giving and serving others. It inspired one of my favorite family traditions. On Christmas Eve, we get a bunch of gift cards and hand them out to people. Sometimes we give in secret and hide to watch the reactions. We have left gift cards on bus-stop benches and laundromats, a teddy bear in a discount store shopping cart, and money at a gas station pump. Each gift is left with a note saying, "Merry Christmas! Jesus loves you! Enjoy or Share." It is so fun watching unsuspecting people find surprises, given in Jesus's name. We also often keep bags filled with snacks, water bottles, socks, restaurant gift cards, and hotel toiletries in our car to hand out the window to homeless people we see on street corners.

If your student isn't serving in some form, consider mailing them gift cards or "goodie bags" to give away with their friends in a fun way. That might get them kickstarted to do more with their own funds. Another option is to offer an incentive. Maybe give extra spending or gas money in exchange for a few hours serving in the homeless shelter. Once your student starts, she likely will want to return on her own.

Just how Jesus served others, we are instructed to serve, too. Look online for a multitude of Bible verses about serving. Today, pray that your child will be a servant of God and will serve His people humbly and willingly.

Lord, please help _____ to have a servant heart. Help her to serve those around her who are in need, even if it is just a listening ear. If there are ways that I can encourage her to serve, give me the resources and suggestions to which she will be most open. When she does serve, help her to feel satisfaction and a desire to serve again. In Jesus's name, amen.

Day 15

"Whatever you do, work heartily, as for the Lord and not for men, knowing that from the Lord you will receive the inheritance as your reward. You are serving the Lord Christ."
~ Colossians 3:23-24 ~

HOMEWORK

In high school, homework is a dreaded, yet everyday part of all students' lives. After going to school for seven hours a day, they often are assigned work to do at home that takes another couple of hours to complete. When students enter college, they immediately have a sense of freedom. Parents can no longer demand they do their homework before going out. It may take college freshmen an adjustment period to figure out that their grades will be affected if they don't do their assignments. I remember my first college test as a freshman. I did well in high school and could manage to get A's by cramming the night before. It was a disappointing realization when I sat down at ten o'clock the night before my college American Government test to start reading the chapters for the first time — all six of them! Not only had I not read ahead of time when it was assigned, but I hadn't even noticed that it was six chapters instead of two or three. I was not prepared, and unless I had a photographic memory (I do not), I was not going to do well. You would think I learned for the next test. Nope. I was way too used to procrastinating with a positive outcome. It took me the entire semester to catch on to how to correctly take notes and study as I read little by little instead of trying to do it all at once the night before. My grades suffered, but I learned my lesson the hard way and did much better after that.

As parents, we spend so many years telling our kids to do their homework, that we can sometimes forget that they may put the pressure on themselves to do what needs to be done. Every kid is different. I have a daughter who is a typical example of an overachiever. In college she was working towards a double major and double minor and since she was a music major, she was required to put in many hours of rehearsals and lessons, as well as keep up with the regular academic rigor. She graduated with a 4.0 but was the type of student that I repeatedly had to tell that it was okay to miss an assignment occasionally so that she could relax briefly.

When it comes to homework, or any kind of work, our prayer should be that our kids do their best but still have time and energy to keep God first. Of course, we want our kids to succeed, but if they are using their talents that God has given them to the best of their abilities, then He will use them wherever and however He wants.

Lord, please give _____ the desire to do his schoolwork diligently and to not procrastinate. Help him to do his best and still put You first in all things. Allow his hard work to be reflected in his grades so he isn't discouraged. In Jesus's name, amen.

Day 16

"Then the Lord God said, "It is not good that the man sh\. make him a helper fit for him."
~ *Genesis 2:18* ~

LONELINESS

God did not intend for any of us to be alone. He designed us to have friends and families and conversations and company. There are plenty of animals that are considered solitary because they naturally are alone most of the time, but humans are not meant to be completely alone. Because of that, we can suffer from loneliness when we are by ourselves. Our college kids may feel lonely away, as we feel lonely at home without them.

When each of my kids went off to college, I had a sense of unexplainable loneliness. When the first one ventured off to a different state, I was surrounded by my husband and five kids at home, but he was the first to leave, and milestones are always extra emotional for me. It took me a few weeks, and I missed him, but I got over the lonely feeling in the pit of my stomach. Two years later, my daughter headed off to college. She was only an hour and a half away, so I hoped it would be a little easier, but I still felt lonely. I had three teens and a pre-teen still at home, so I certainly was not alone. After another two years, my second son left for Virginia, followed by my third son a year later. My two girls, who are still at home with my husband and I, also miss having the whole family together. It is normal to be sad about life changes, if you don't dwell on them and are able to eventually accept the new normal.

When I am feeling sorry for myself, one of the best ways for me to snap out of it is to talk to or pray for someone else who is struggling with something similar. That reminds me that I am not the only one going through it. Pray for the other parents who are feeling the same loneliness that you are. Connecting with them also will help. When my fourth kid was a senior in high school, a group of parents met regularly for breakfast. We even had a name— MOGS (Mothers of Graduating Seniors— dads were welcome, too, though). It was a wonderful support during and after that

ar. Find parents of other college freshmen and support one

When you are feeling lonely with your new college freshman gone, try to think of how she must be feeling, too. She is in a temporary home without any family. When you are missing her, perhaps she is feeling the same way about you. Give her a call. Pray extra hard for her today to feel a sense of belonging in her new surroundings and to not feel alone amid the large crowds.

Lord, please fill the void I am feeling and help my loneliness subside. Help me to reach out to other parents of college kids for support. Please help _____ feel Your presence and not feel lonely. Help her surround herself with people and develop positive relationships. In Jesus's name, amen.

Day 17

"He who loves money will not be satisfied with money, nor he who loves wealth with his income; this also is vanity."
~ *Ecclesiastes 5:10* ~

MONEY

There is a humorous saying that MOM stands for Made Of Money and DAD is for Dollars At Disposal. If you haven't felt as if that adequately represents you yet, just wait. It will. Here is funny correspondence to which most college parents can relate:

Dear Dad,

$chool i$ really great. I am making lot$ of friend$ and $tudying very hard. I $imply can't think of anything I need, $o if you would like, you can ju$t $end me a card, a$ I would love to hear from you.

Love,

Your $on

Dear Son,

I kNOw that astroNOmy, ecoNOmics, and oceaNOgraphy are eNOugh to keep even an hoNOr student busy. Do NOt forget that the pursuit of kNOwledge is a NOble task, and you can never study eNOugh.

Love,

Dad

It's fun to joke about college kids needing money, but the reality is that figuring out spending and saving can be overwhelming for them, especially if they relied on you for most of their spending money at home. Even their "dining dollars" or "campus cash" aren't unlimited and they will need to learn how to budget so they aren't overindulging at the beginning of the week and hungry when Saturday comes. If your child doesn't have a job yet, a campus job next semester might be a good option. They usually don't require transportation, and students can work around their class schedules.

It may take you and your freshman a semester or two to figure out how much money he will need and the amount you are contributing, if any. Encourage your student to divide his earned money immediately into tithe, spending, and savings. Of course, it would be helpful if he can further budget the spending and savings into sub-categories, but if not, he'll eventually learn that when the money is gone, it's gone — unless you are the type of parent who responds to the above letter with:

Dear Son,
YESterday, I received your letter. It was the graYESt of days before I read it. Since I hate goodbYES and have been thinking of you off at college with those blue eYES and favorite polYESter soccer shirt, I wanted to respond before Dad. He still has the drYESt sense of humor.
Love,
Mom

Lord, guide _____ *to be a good steward with his money. Please provide the necessary resources so he can have what he needs. Help him to feel the nudging of the Holy Spirit to tithe from his income. Help him to save wisely and give generously. In Jesus's name, amen.*

Day 18

"He who gathers in summer is a prudent son, but he who sleeps in harvest is a son who brings shame."
~ Proverbs 10:5 ~

ACTIVENESS

If your child is naturally active, then you probably aren't too worried about him being a couch potato during all his free time; but if your student is the type to sit around playing video games, scrolling through social media sites, or watching YouTube videos or Netflix, you should make today a day to pray for his activeness each time you think of him. Relaxation is perfectly acceptable and needed, but if laziness trumps activeness, our students will suffer.

I mentioned previously about the great dorms at Union University. As much as the students loved them, there was concern from my husband and I about the solitude of the students. At many colleges, freshmen are housed in dorms with lots of students in a hall, sharing a bathroom and common living area. They have activities geared for people on each floor or building and students often leave their doors open, allowing for them to easily meet new people. There is more motivation to get up and get active when invited to do so, especially for sedentary people. At UU, however, it's much easier for students to remain in their rooms, so I prayed a lot that my son would get out.

Most campuses have weight rooms, basketball and volleyball courts, and many opportunities for students to play intramural sports. If your student had a favorite sport he played in high school but doesn't want to play so competitively in college, an intramural sport is a great alternative. Students compete against other teams from the same school, and it is much less pressure than playing for the university. It is also always an option for students to just play pick-up games of various sports with other students.

My sons took up disc golf as a hobby in high school. If you aren't familiar with it, it is a cross between Frisbee and golf. It involves discs that are aimed towards baskets that are far away. When my sons went to college, they brought their discs with them. One of them joined the school's disc golf team and the others continued to play for fun. When they would come home from college, they would play with my husband, aiming at random things at the nearby park. I wanted to join in on the quality time, so they taught me how to play. I am terrible at it, but I love their company and being outdoors, so I just try to ignore that my discs go half as far as theirs. Consider sending your student an active game to play with suitemates. Kan Jam, Spikeball, and disc golf are all popular among college students, and most would welcome them in their mailboxes. When your student comes home for the summer, he can teach you how to play so you'll both stay active.

◆ ◆ ◆

Lord, thank You for all the choices _____ has for staying active. Help him to choose a healthy balance between relaxing and moving. Lead him to activities which he will enjoy so he will return to them.
In Jesus's name, amen.

Day 19

"And let us consider how to stir up one another to love and good works, not neglecting to meet together, as is the habit of some, but encouraging one another, and all the more as you see the Day drawing near."

~ *Hebrews 10:24-25* ~

CHURCH

Recent studies have shown a huge percentage of students — up to 70 percent — abandon church and their faith once they leave home for college. Those are particularly disturbing statistics for parents who raised their kids attending weekly church services, Sunday school, and youth group activities. After doing some research, however, I felt a little better about it. Yes, young adults are leaving their faith and churches, but the statistics have been grouped together and many students are simply leaving mainstream churches in search of more intimate settings.

With society constantly changing, churches also adapt to the preferences of people attending. When I was in school, we sang hymns with a choir wearing robes, and the minister, also in a robe, preached. His only visual aid was his Bible. He would then sit in a reserved chair behind the pulpit next to the associate pastor who, you guessed it, donned a robe. There weren't moving lights, videos, full instrumental bands, or audio equipment echoing throughout the sanctuary. It was difficult for new people to attend without being noticed and warmly greeted. Potluck lunches and dinners were a normal part of Sunday afternoons and everyone knew each other's prayer requests. Many of today's college students grew up in large churches with contemporary music and entertaining services, where shorts and flip-flops are accepted attire.

Have a conversation with your child about what kind of church she is comfortable attending and offer to look up reviews of some near the university. Sometimes young adults have a desire to go to church but don't want to take the time to research them. If transportation is an issue, find one that offers rides to and from campus. There are a lot that do that.

Be cognizant that in the Bible, the church is not a building. The church is the people. In 1 Timothy 5, Paul describes the church as people who are dedicated to serving others. God intends for your freshman to go to church, but that means meeting with a group of fellow Christians and teaching, serving, and preaching. Whether your child finds a traditional church, mega-church, or non-traditional church doesn't matter if Christ is the head of it and she can relate, serve, and grow closer to Him.

Lord, help _____ find a church where she can get plugged in and serve others, worship You, and fellowship with other Christians. If there is some way that I can help her find a church without overstepping my bounds, guide me to those steps. In Jesus's name, amen.

Day 20

"And God said, 'Behold, I have given you every plant yielding seed that is on the face of all the earth, and every tree with seed in its fruit. You shall have them for food.'"

~ Genesis 1:29 ~

FOOD

Ask anyone to tell you the first words that come to mind when college food is mentioned, and you will likely hear "Ramen noodles" as the reply. They are inexpensive, easy to cook in a microwave, and somewhat tasty and filling. What more could a college student ask for? When I was in college, my affordable food of choice was broccoli-cheddar rice. The broccoli was probably freeze-dried, but at least I was getting my vegetables, right?

The first time my youngest daughter went to a buffet-style restaurant, she was so excited about all the unhealthy food options that were all-you-can-eat, that she indulged to her heart's content and then got very sick a few hours later. College kids on meal plans remind me of her, as they try all their favorites. It's exciting to have foods at their disposal that Mom and Dad didn't have at home or only allowed for special treats. This is a probable cause of the "freshman fifteen."

Lack of time can be a reason that students do not eat well. All of mine had difficulties making it to the cafeteria before breakfast closed. I'm not sure why we included that meal in the plan — probably because we hoped they would use it. My daughter lived close enough to home that she would visit many weekends. Her favorite grab-and-go breakfast food was pancakes so I would send her back with large baggies full of homemade ones for her to quickly microwave and eat on her way to class.

As parents, we have reasons to be concerned. Some students don't get enough variety so are lacking in nutrients from different food groups, and still others suffer because they just don't have enough food. Eating disorders, such as anorexia and bulimia, are prevalent among college students due to acceptance and appearance issues. Many students can't afford to buy food, so they skip meals, sometimes sacrificing food money to pay for books, school supplies, or outings with friends. Allergies can be another factor for being concerned about students' food intake.

What is a parent to do? Talk (or text) to your child about what and where she has been eating. I'd advise doing it in a way that is conversational and not confrontational, avoiding any judgements about the food choices, or you won't get any future answers about the subject. If you know she is lacking food money, perhaps send some gift cards to nearby restaurants. Sending a box of food is a huge hit with college kids. Include nutritional food with a yummy homemade treat. If you send enough to share, you'll bring a smile to her roommate, too. If you lack the funds to assist, be aware that most colleges have food pantries on campus, so direct her there. Be ready to make your child's favorite homecooked meal when she visits. I can assure you, she is eagerly awaiting it.

Lord, help _____ to make healthy and wise choices about food. Prevent her from becoming malnourished or hungry, yet help her to not overindulge, either. In Jesus's name, amen.

Day 21

"Everyone must submit to governing authorities. For all authority comes from God, and those in positions of authority have been placed there by God."

~ *Romans 13:1* ~

OBEDIENCE

When my kids were little, my husband and I expected them to follow the family rules. I had studied behavior modification and knew about empty threats and positive reinforcements. If they didn't obey, there were consequences, usually involving sitting in the time-out room or losing a privilege or reward. We had a system that worked well for us involving a chart, stars, and checkmarks that we used from the time they were toddlers all the way through high school. The kids were allowed three warnings a day with no consequences, but after that they got checkmarks and started losing privileges. If they never got more than three warnings, they were rewarded at the end of the week with a prize, which progressed to dollars when they were older. Checkmarks resulted in not getting to choose a book to read before bed. As they got older, it was adapted and became losing WiFi for the day. Having a couple strong-willed kids who didn't mind not getting rewarded, we had to add one more step of having to do a small chore for each checkmark. On more than one occasion, we were told by a couple kids that it wasn't fair to still be required to do the punishment chore once an apology was given. We explained to them that they are forgiven, but in the real world, there are rules to follow and consequences if they aren't followed. If they steal, they will go to jail. In jail, they will still have to do their work detail no matter how sorry they are. Hopefully our college kids will remember the lessons we taught them repeatedly.

Peer pressure is a huge part of college kids' lives but since they are adults now, we can only pray that they will feel the tugging of the Holy Spirit to obey authorities' rules and laws. When one of my sons was a freshman, he went with some friends to a very old, abandoned mental hospital that was rumored to be haunted. He was concerned about going into the building since he knew it would be trespassing, so he was the lookout person. He told me later that he would never do something like that again because he was so worried about getting caught.

My kids like hearing my story from when I was in college and some friends took me to build a bonfire in what we thought was a permissible place. When we heard sirens and saw lights of fire trucks, we quickly put out the fire and got out of there fast, realizing they were coming to us. We probably all have memories of a college adventure involving a lack of obedience and judgement. Our kids will learn from theirs just as we did from ours. Let's just hope it doesn't involve work detail.

Lord, guide _____ to follow authority and obey the rules of the college, as well as any laws. Help him to feel the Holy Spirit leading him away when faced with a choice to join others in disobedience. If he does break rules and getting caught will protect him, allow that to happen. In Jesus's name, amen.

Day 22

"'I have said these things to you, that in me you may have peace. In the world you will have tribulation. But take heart; I have overcome the world.'"

~ John 16:33 ~

PEACE

Because of all the pressures on young adults, it isn't surprising they are in turmoil. With college comes responsibilities and expectations. Students are required to think daily about grades, jobs, money, friends, and a multitude of other things when only a month or two earlier, they were at home playing video games while their parents did their laundry and cooked for them.

College campuses are notorious for protests. Everything from religion, to human and animal rights, to the existence of UFOs is debated. Students regularly encounter yelling, arguing and distension because of all the different opinions being voiced. When I was a freshman at the University of Central Florida, I remember everybody talking about a guy who periodically stood with a loudspeaker in the middle of campus yelling at students passing by for the way they dressed or walked or styled their hair. It was humiliating, yet crowds would gather to watch the ruckus.

Our students are exposed to constant disarray in the world in most of the platforms in which they engage. Video games and movies involve shooting and attacks. When turning on the television to the major news stations, it is common to hear multiple "experts" shouting all at once about how their opinions are the correct ones. Social media is filled with bashing those who think differently. Even a simple question posted on a public forum can quickly have many negative responses, attacking the inquirer. Nations are at war, politicians are fighting, people everywhere are bullying, there are shootings at schools and malls, and spiritual battles are surrounding us.

Take a moment and read Psalm 46 today and meditate on its words. The world is in chaos, but God is the refuge for your student and will bring her strength and help. If children are not at peace, their parents are not at peace. If you have a feeling that your child is in turmoil, consider texting her John 14:27. "Peace I leave with you; my peace I give you. I do not give to you as the world gives. Do not let your hearts be troubled and do not be afraid." It may be the encouragement she is seeking today. Most importantly, pray for her peace. God can deliver it to her...and to you.

Lord, I know that You are the only source of true peace in this chaotic world. Help _____ to be surrounded by Your perfect peace as she faces turmoil today. Allow me to feel Your comforting peace as I think of her. Help us both be still and know that You are God. In Jesus's name, amen.

Day 23

"He will not let your foot be moved; he who keeps you will not slumber."
~ Psalm 121:3 ~

SAFETY

As soon as my children were born, I felt a responsibility to protect them. It began with swaddling them securely and insisting visitors wash hands. My infants were placed in car seats with multiple buckles. When they first rolled over, I was careful not to leave them alone on beds. Crawling little ones meant making sure no small pieces were on the floor. With newly walking toddlers came swimming pool gates, cabinet locks, shades' ropes shortened, door knobs secured, and bathtubs drained. As they grew, my husband and I required helmets and knee pads, sunscreen, bug repellent, shin guards, and life jackets to be worn. As hard as we tried to keep them safe, we still managed to have kids with broken bones, stitches, sunburns, bug bites, bumps, bruises, scrapes, and water up the nose.

Just because my kids turn eighteen or leave for college, doesn't mean I suddenly no longer have the desire to keep them safe. I struggled immensely with this at first, because they no longer wanted or really needed me to anymore. After all, they are adults. I have learned, though, that even though they don't need my protection at this stage in their lives, they do still need me to care about their safety and to support and love them if they are hurt.

My oldest son bought a car his junior year of college, so he packed up and drove from Tennessee to Florida by himself for the first time. My Mama's intuition was feeling very uneasy. Several hours into his trip, he called to tell me he was okay, but had just had a car accident. Yikes! I couldn't prevent the accident, but I could help him figure out how to handle insurance, get his car fixed, and get home. My daughter called me the first night she was away as a new freshman to tell me how upset she was because a girl had been injured badly during an ice-breaker game when a hook went into her arm. The possibility of being injured while away

51

from home became a reality and she relied on me for comfort. One of my sons hurt himself repeatedly his first year of college. Somebody fell on him while playing football, causing his glasses to break and cut his eye. He sent me a picture of blood running down his face. Another time, he was longboarding with his roommate down a hill and they collided, hitting the street and a parked car. He sent me a picture of road-burned arms and torso and legs...and more blood. I didn't like that he was hurt, but I loved that he told me immediately and knew I would sincerely care. My other son cut his finger to the nerve opening a box. I couldn't convince him to go to urgent care because he was headed out for opening night of a new Star Wars movie, but I was glad he called so I knew to pray for him. Be content when your child shares his hurts and follow up and ask how he is doing. Remember that Jesus is the real protector, not you.

Lord, please keep _____ safe and free from severe injury. Help him contact me if he gets hurt and know that I honestly care. As his ultimate protector, please keep him safe in Your arms. In Jesus's name, amen.

Day 24

"Fear not, for I am with you; be not dismayed, for I am your God; I will strengthen you, I will help you, I will uphold you with my righteous right hand."

~ Isaiah 41:10 ~

HEALTH

Helpless was how I felt when my kids got sick while they were away at school. I wanted to bring them medicine, take their temperatures, and give them cold rags, but all I could do was offer a comforting voice and prayers. Chances are that at some point during her stay at college, your child will become ill. Take comfort in knowing most universities have a clinic or nurse available on campus. The Resident Assistants are also there to monitor the well-being of your student and should offer to get meals from the cafeteria to bring back to the dorm, if needed. Students are permitted to miss classes when they aren't well, and most will gladly stay in bed when not up to attending. A couple of my kids weren't aware of those resources, so be sure to direct yours to where the help is. If your child didn't bring a variety of medicines with her, consider sending her some so she has them if the need arises.

Not only do we want our kids to be physically healthy, we also want them to be healthy mentally and emotionally. Unfortunately, mental disorders are on the rise among college students, so parents need to be aware of the symptoms and know where to point their students for help. According to the Center for Collegiate Mental Health, one in five university students is suffering from anxiety or depression. Social media and technology contribute to impaired social interactions, which play a role, along with lack of sleep, homesickness, and concerns about grades and money. Many students don't seek help they need because they aren't aware it's available, so talk about it now in case she needs it later.

Also, discuss with your student mental health treatment options. A friend of mine told me about her student who was given anti-depressant medication when he visited the campus clinic. There was little counseling offered first. She learned that many of her son's friends at the same college were also prescribed anti-depressants. At first, I thought that must be how they handle the emotional problems of students at that university, but then I researched it and was alarmed to discover how prevalent those types of medications are across colleges nationwide. It will help your student to know now that medications can be beneficial, but should only be taken as a last resort, since they often have side effects and are difficult to stop taking.

You have access to the resources at your child's campus. Call or look online before a problem arises so that when your student reaches out to you, she can be pointed in the right direction. If you don't have her roommate's phone number yet, ask for it or an RA's number in case of an emergency. You may be separated, but you have the power of prayer, and God is the greatest Healer of all.

Lord, help _____ to stay well, physically, mentally, and emotionally. If she needs taken care of, please send someone to her who will assist. Help her learn how to prevent mental and physical disorders and to trust You as her Healer if she gets sick. In Jesus's name, amen.

Day 25

"Without counsel plans fail, but with many advisers they succeed."
~ Proverbs 15:22 ~

MENTOR

Even though the word mentor isn't mentioned in the Bible, the concept is seen throughout it. Relationships were built within small groups and the older and wiser people guided the younger ones. It is beneficial for young adults to have a mentor to whom they can relate who is not a parent. That is difficult for me to grasp because I want to be the one my kids come to for advice. I sometimes need reminded that my husband and I certainly don't know everything, and our kids will be much more well-rounded if they learn from others. There were many times while they were growing up when they would excitedly share about something new they had learned from a teacher at school that I had already taught them. I remember my mom saying the exact thing about my sisters and I. God intends for us to learn from various people, especially about Him. We probably all remember being taught a lesson in school that we didn't understand at first, but then had a different teacher explain it another way, and the concept "clicked."

I wish I could say that I told each of my kids to find a mentor when they went off to college, but it was actually my oldest son who taught me the importance of it. He was struggling with some issues that most college students face and had been told by a wise professor about the need for a mentor. Fortunately, he had formed relationships with a couple Christian male professors, and they took time to meet with him regularly. When I listened to my son tell me on a phone call about how he talked to his mentors about his struggles, my first reaction was to wonder why he didn't come to my husband or I first. After I hung up, however, I gave it some more thought. I had a house full of teenagers and had lots of experience with them thinking we have little knowledge about what we know to be true. It's part of growing up. Young people want to find things out for themselves, and if that comes from the same source it has since they were born, it isn't their own understanding. My son was beyond the rebellious stage, but the same principle applied. He needed to relate to different people who he knew would not judge him and might offer advice and different perspectives than what he would expect from his parents. I understood and was thankful he had reached out to me at all.

In the Bible, Jethro mentored Moses. Moses mentored Joshua. Eli mentored Samuel. Samuel mentored David. David mentored Solomon. Elijah mentored Elisha. Mordecai mentored Esther. Jesus mentored the apostles. Those are just a few examples. Encourage your student to find a mentor who is a trustworthy follower of Christ.

Lord, please put at least one mentor into _____'s life who can share Christian perspectives and listen well. Open _____'s heart and mind to seeking a mentor while away from home and to not hold back if a discussion will be beneficial for him. In Jesus's name, amen.

Day 26

"Therefore, since we are surrounded by so great a cloud of witnesses, let us also lay aside every weight, and sin which clings so closely, and let us run with endurance the race that is set before us, looking to Jesus, the founder and perfecter of our faith, who for the joy that was set before him endured the cross, despising the shame, and is seated at the right hand of the throne of God."
~ Hebrews 12:1 ~

PERSEVERANCE

Albert Einstein didn't start speaking until the age of four or reading until he was seven. Theodor Seuss Geisel, better known as Dr. Seuss, had his first book rejected 27 times by publishers. Before Walt Disney created the magical world named for him, his early newspaper editor told him that he "lacked imagination and had no good ideas." Thomas Edison obtained more than 1,000 patents after his teachers told him he was "too stupid to learn anything." Oprah Winfrey was fired from her first TV job. Basketball legend, Michael Jordan, was cut from his high school basketball team. Vincent Van Gogh only managed to sell one painting during his lifetime. Sir James Dyson failed 5,126 times before creating a successful prototype of the now popular bagless vacuum cleaner.

Nobody wants to fail, and no parent wishes failure upon his child, but like Albert Einstein once said, "If you've never failed, you've never tried anything new." It can be intimidating for a young adult to venture into a challenging academic class, play a sport for a university, or perform a solo in front of a large audience. He might earn a poor grade, fumble the ball, or freeze with stage fright. However, with perseverance, determination, practice, and Jesus by his side, he can discover how to pass with honors, master the sport, or face an even bigger crowd with a standing ovation.

Take heart if your freshman has setbacks and pray that he can use them to move ahead further and grow closer to the Lord, while gaining knowledge from his experiences. Learning how to utilize those hindrances now will benefit him greatly when he graduates and faces even bigger challenges. Your child will be taught new ideas from his college professors, but experience is where those concepts are put into play. It is a requirement for many college majors to have an internship before graduating, allowing for a time of learning by doing. When you are looking for a new physician, home builder, or mechanic, you probably research the number of years in business. Rarely is perfection expected without practice. Our children may not be famous or drastically fail at their professions before making millions, but they will make mistakes and they will learn from them, just like we did.

Lord, when _____ makes mistakes, help him to learn and grow from them. Also, please help him to grow closer to You through any trials he may face. Give him the strength and energy to persevere in any situation in which You can teach Him. In Jesus's name, amen.

Day 27

"Do not be conformed to this world, but be transformed by the renewal of your mind, that by testing you may discern what is the will of God, what is good and acceptable and perfect."

~ Romans 12:12 ~

PARTYING

Partying and college are known to go together. Popular spring break destinations are inundated with college students notorious for shenanigans while drunk or high. Movies about colleges seem to always include the partying lifestyle. It's as if drinking, casual sex, and drugs are expected of college kids. For many freshmen, it is the first time they are living without parents telling them what they can and can't do. Peer pressure is extremely strong, and they want to belong and not to be ridiculed, so some succumb to the pressures and join in with what is perceived as normal. Even at Christian colleges, my children tell me about the commonness of students smoking weed and getting drunk. Today, pray that your student will not give in to those pressures.

My freshman year of college, I joined a sorority and was expected to go to "socials." We were given the proper lectures about how nobody should drink if underage and that we should maintain their high standards, remain classy, and not behave in a way that could make the sorority or ourselves look bad. I was relieved that it wouldn't be like all the stories I thought to be true about parties. Then, I went to my first social. It didn't take long for people to become drunk. Having never been around that before, I felt very uncomfortable, especially because lots of the people there were under the legal drinking age. I watched many of them do things that put them in danger, including driving. Having lost childhood friends in high school as the result of drunk driving, I knew first-hand the negative effects of too much alcohol and wanted to do something to help. My second semester, I became president of Greeks Advocating Mature Management of Alcohol (GAMMA). I convinced myself it was okay to go to the parties if I didn't drink so I could be a designated driver. I always responded with "I don't drink" when offered alcohol, so I wouldn't be asked twice, and I never carried an open cup of water or soda to avoid any unwanted drugs getting slipped in a drink. I tried to teach other students the same tricks, but it was difficult to find any who cared. After going home at the end of my first year of college and reflecting on my social life and spiritual walk, I felt convicted by the Holy Spirit to stay away from any parties with alcohol. It was like a huge weight was lifted off my shoulders, as I was transformed by the renewal of my mind, discerning the will of God. The next year, I discovered other parties with nothing illegal or uncomfortable, and formed meaningful relationships. The peer pressure was gone, and I could be who God wanted me to be.

Our students should know it is okay to be different than "typical." They need to understand their worth is not based on how popular they are or how many shots they consume. They should recognize that deep friendships are formed by discussions and quality time. Even if they start on the popular path, God can guide them back to the road that is different than the world's.

Lord, put it on _____'s heart to follow You first. Help her to avoid any situations where she might feel pressured to engage in illegal or immoral behavior. Help her to abstain from drugs and alcohol and any actions that are displeasing to You. In Jesus's name, amen.

Day 28

"You make known to me the path of life; in your presence there is fullness of joy; at your right hand are pleasures forevermore."
~ *Psalm 16:11* ~

ADVENTURES

If your child hasn't told you yet about an upcoming trip, he will eventually. Most college students decide at some point to explore outside the boundaries of their dorm rooms. Notice I used the word "told" and not "asked." He may even tell you after the escapade instead of beforehand since he no longer must report to you every time he leaves, like he probably did at home. With freedom, comes a sense of adventure.

My kids have travelled to friends' houses a couple of hours away from campus, across several states, and even to other countries during their college years. I had so many questions that I couldn't get answered ahead of time like I could when they lived at home. Will the parents be home? Do you have enough gas? How can you afford that? Did you bring water? Ask away, but be prepared for answers that might be different than you hoped they would be.

Your student may decide to explore sights near his new home-away-from-home. All my sons loved hiking in the woods owned by their universities. They also took road trips a little further away. One of them developed a love for backpacking and went many times on day trips to nearby mountains. As I am writing this sentence, he is on his way to Texas from Orlando with friends to hike in Big Bend National Park.

Don't assume your child will limit his adventures to The United Sates. Many colleges offer studying abroad options, mission trip opportunities, or internships in other countries. One of my college-age sons recently returned from Italy with a friend's family. Another son interned at a church during summer break, allowing him to travel to Africa and Haiti. I doubt those will be the last of my children's overseas excursions.

This is the best time for your student to travel, since he is single, doesn't have kids in tow, and has minimal financial responsibilities. He may not have the adventurous opportunities in the future that he does now or the ability to get up and go without many resources again. If he is going on road-trips to stay with friends' families, consider it a blessing that there are families nearby who can look out for him and welcome him with open arms. He might not even want to explore beyond the perimeters of his college, but God's will may be different. If God is putting it on his heart, join in encouraging him to explore His world.

Lord, lead _____ on adventures that will bring him closer to You. Allow him to feel Your presence wherever he goes and to follow Your will as he makes decisions about places to go and people to visit. Help keep him safe as he ventures out beyond his college, and help me and him to trust that You are with him anywhere in this world of Yours. In Jesus's name, amen.

Day 29

"I have taught you the way of wisdom; I have led you in the paths of uprightness."
~ *Proverbs 4:11* ~

PROFESSORS

In elementary school, middle school, and even high school, parents are welcomed and expected to meet their children's teachers. There is a time for questions and an opportunity for the students and parents to learn what to expect. If only it were that way in college! It is possible to meet some professors while on a college tour, but it is usually just the department chair and one or two other professors. For the last 13 years, you have been able to let your teacher know your child's strengths and weaknesses and if he has any special requirements to enhance his learning. You could voice if he was an audio, visual, or kinesthetic learner. Now, as he blends in with the other students, you can no longer tell the teacher how wonderful he is or that he is a little shy at first. What's a mother to do? Pray! God's got this and so does your freshman!

My son and daughter each had a positive experience with professors when they were visiting their colleges. My husband took my son to visit Union University so that he could inquire about their digital media program. When they went to find the department chair, he was on his way out to lunch and invited my son and my husband to join him and his colleague. They were able to answer questions and converse, and my son was able to see that they were real people and not intimidating at all. When my daughter visited Southeastern University, she was unsure whether she should major in piano, voice, or theater. She met with the theater professor and explained that she was torn between the options, knowing that each required lots of time and dedication. The professor listened and then told her that God had given her talents and she shouldn't let any of them be wasted. He explained that the professors in the different areas she was considering would collaborate to make it work so she could study them all. Wow! Exactly what she needed.

Unfortunately, not all professors have the students' best interests in mind. They may want only a few students to pass their classes. Some are inappropriate, unapproachable, boring, or difficult to understand. There are professors who force their viewpoints as the only correct ones to the students. Several years ago, a student at a Florida college made headlines when he refused to stomp on a paper with the word "Jesus" written on it. His professor suspended him from the class. While that is an extreme case, your student will probably have a professor at some point who is a source of conflict. For each one who is questionable, however, there will be many trustworthy professors with whom he can have meaningful discussions.

Asking your new freshman about his professors will initiate conversations about them and allow you to get to know something about them. Remind him that he should not be wary of talking to his professors and that he should reach out to them if he has any problems or questions. Pray that your student will be discerning. Although he should be respectful to his professors, he should also stand up for God above all else.

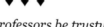

Lord, please help _____'s professors be trustworthy and have the students' best interests in mind. Help _____ to get along with them and adjust to their teaching styles. Give him the courage to stand up for his beliefs if they are ever compromised. In Jesus's name, amen.

Day 30

"My people will abide in a peaceful habitation, in secure dwellings, and in quiet resting places."
~ Isaiah 32:18 ~

HOME

When my daughter got married, she gave me a water bottle that says, "Home is where the mom is." It reminds me that the distance between my kids and I won't alter the bonds we share. My oldest son got married shortly after getting his bachelor's degree, so he never moved back to Florida like I had anticipated when he left as a freshman. Knowing that once kids leave, they don't always return home as expected, I was relieved when my daughter attended school less than two hours away, and I cried a few extra tears when my younger sons went out of state to college. I always look forward to when they come home.

Regardless of where God leads her once she gets her degree, your child will return home many times while in college. Nobody warned me that the first few visits home would not be the bed of roses I was awaiting, so consider yourself warned. My kids were never permitted food in the carpeted rooms, including their bedrooms. Each family member is to use only one drink cup a day and is expected to rinse dirty dishes. Laundry goes into the dirty clothes basket daily, not stock-piled on bedroom floors. If leaving, say good-bye and give the approximate return time. When my children came home for college breaks, I would find unrinsed dishes in bedrooms and socks strewn throughout the house. Empty, used cups seemed to multiply and ended up on surfaces that should never be wet. Unfolded blankets and pillows were frequently left on the couch. I'd look for my kids and discover they had left the house. At first, I was so excited just to have them back home that I picked up the messes, washed the laundry, rinsed the dishes, and ignored the broken house rules. I didn't want them mad at me when they were only home for a short time.

Your student's intention is not to break the rules. She has gotten used to using her bed as a kitchen table and her floor as a laundry basket. She has been able to use as many glasses as she wishes in a day. She's been placing dirty dishes into a bin without even rinsing them. She hasn't had to tell anyone where she is going. It is best to address expectations with your child before she comes home, preventing discord once she's there. Consider listing them on a shared iPhone Note or Google Doc, with an invitation to collaborate and a positive note. Include that it's just a friendly reminder to follow the house rules when she comes home, since you know she has been doing things differently on her own. Ask if she thinks they are fair or would like to talk about any of the rules.

When our kids are home for long weekends, my husband and I treat them like guests. I cook their favorite meals and we excuse them from helping with dishes. For the longer breaks, they are expected to act at home as they did before they left for college. I love having them home and always will, no matter their ages and stages whether they follow the rules or not. Home may be where the mom is, and I'm great with that as long as I'm not home with empty rooms for long.

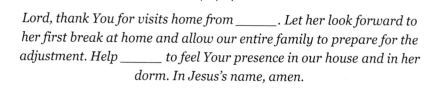

Lord, thank You for visits home from _____. Let her look forward to her first break at home and allow our entire family to prepare for the adjustment. Help _____ to feel Your presence in our house and in her dorm. In Jesus's name, amen.

I'd love to hear from you! Email me at jena@lettinggolettinggod.com.

Thank you to my amazing and supportive family.

David and Nana, your first reads meant so much to me.

Gramps and Grammie, I appreciate you advertising.

Jaci, thank you for turning the tables and proofing. I wouldn't have finished without you.

Thank you, Jesus, for putting this on my heart and nudging me to finish. I give You the glory!

Made in the USA
Las Vegas, NV
10 August 2021

27904690R00039